HISTORY OF HAITI

ESTHER ROSE ALEXANDRA VERNE

Copyright © 2025 by Esther Rose Alexandra Verne

All rights are reserved, and no part of this publication may be reproduced, distributed, or transmitted in any manner, whether through photocopying, recording, or any other electronic or mechanical methods, without the explicit prior written permission of the publisher. This restriction applies to any form or means of reproduction or distribution.

Exceptions to this rule include brief quotations that may be incorporated into critical reviews, as well as certain other noncommercial uses that are allowed by copyright law. Any such usage must adhere to the specified conditions and permissions outlined by the copyright holder.

Book Design by HMDPublishing.com

DEDICATION

To
Alexandre P. Angrand, Rubby, Abigaelle Toussaint Kevin and karl Joseph, Paige, and Zahir Alexandre

This book is for you.
May you always walk with pride, knowing the strength of your roots and the richness of your heritage.
Within these pages are the stories I wish you—and every Haitian child—could grow up hearing.
Stories of resistance, brilliance, hope, and freedom.
Stories that show who we are, where we come from, and why Haiti will always matter.

You are the future.
May the past inspire you to dream boldly, stand tall, and carry the legacy forward.

With all my love,
—*Esther R Alexandra Verne*

"Yon sèl dwèt pa manje kalalou."
(*One finger alone can't eat okra.*)
— Haitian Proverb

A reminder that together, we are stronger—and it is through unity that we thrive.

CONTENTS

Introduction 6
1. A New Chapter 8
2. A Divided Island 10
3. The Fight For Freedom 14
4. The Polish Heroes.. 18
5. The Bigger Picture: Freedom Spreads 27
6. The Haitian Flag... 28
7. Haitian History and Important Events 36
8. Treats from Haiti! 43
9. The Haitian Revolution: A Story of Strength and Freedom 50
About the Author 51

Long, long ago, before any other people came to the land we now call Haiti, there were the Taino.

The Taino were peaceful people who lived on the island, growing crops and celebrating life. They called the island Ayti, Quiskeya, and Bohio, which meant *"land of mountains."* They lived in harmony with nature, respecting the world around them.

There were different groups of Taino people, each living in a different area. Every group was led by a special leader called a *"cacique"* (pronounced ka-SEE-keh). A cacique was like a chief or a king who guided the people and made important decisions.

The caciques and their people deeply loved nature. They believed that everything around them the trees, the rain, the animals, and even the moon was full of spirit and life. To them, nature wasn't just something to admire; it was alive with meaning. The gentle rain, the shining moon, and the soft winds were seen as signs of God's love and care.

Each cacique ruled over a certain area of Hayti, and the people gathered around them, living in peace with the land. They respected the mountains, rivers, animals, and plants. The caciques acted as wise protectors, ensuring their people were happy, healthy, and kind to nature.

The Taino believed in a powerful God who was present in everything the sky above, the earth below, the trees that provided food, and the rain that made the crops grow. They did not see God as a person sitting on a cloud but as a presence in all things, even in the stars twinkling at night.

When the rain fell, they saw it as a gift from God. When the moon shone brightly, they believed it was God's way of lighting the darkness. Their love for nature and their faith in God were deeply connected. By caring for the earth, they were also showing respect for God.

INTRODUCTION

Here are some of the most famous caciques (chiefs) from Hayti:

Cacique Bohechío:

Bohechío was a strong and wise leader who ruled over the western part of the island. He made sure his people lived in peace. His niece, Anacaona, later became a famous leader after him.

Cacique Caonabo:

Caonabo was a brave and powerful warrior who defended his people when the Spanish arrived. He fought hard to protect them from being taken over.

Cacique Anacaona:

Anacaona was a smart and kind leader who ruled the Xaragua region. After her husband, Caonabo, passed away, she became the leader. She tried to make peace with the Spanish, but in the end, they captured and treated her unfairly.

Cacique Guarocuya (Enriquillo):

Guarocuya, also known as Enriquillo, was a great leader who fought to protect his people from the Spanish. He is remembered as a hero in both Haiti and the Dominican Republic.

Cacique Hatuey:

Hatuey was a leader from the island of Cuba, but his bravery was remembered throughout the Caribbean. He fought against the Spanish to protect his people. Even though he lived far from Hayti, he became a symbol of resistance for all the islands.

The caciques helped their people live in harmony with the earth and with each other. Their wisdom and strength are still remembered today.

THE ARRIVAL OF STRANGERS

One day, strange ships appeared on the horizon. The Spanish had arrived from across the sea, led by a man named Christopher Columbus. They did not understand the ways of the Taino people and forcefully took control of the land.

The Taino were made to work under harsh conditions, and many of their people were lost. But through it all, they never lost their spirit of unity and strength.

A New Chapter

Haiti was called the *"Pearl of the Caribbean"* because it was a land of great beauty, surrounded by blue waters, and rich in natural treasures. Calling it a *"pearl"* meant it was one of the most precious places in the entire Caribbean!

Both the French and the Spanish wanted to control this island because of its wealth. They wanted the gold and the rich land to make money. The Spanish were the first to take control, but they didn't know how to use the land well. The French saw this and decided to claim part of the island for themselves, knowing it could bring them great fortune.

The French and Spanish fought for control, and in the end, the French won part of the island, which became the French colony of Saint-Domingue (now Haiti). The French turned the land into one of the richest places in the world at the time, but they did so through enslaved labor. People were forced to work on sugar and coffee plantations, making the colony wealthy, but at a terrible cost.

Over time, the Spanish took the northeast of Haiti, while the French expanded their control. The French brought more enslaved people from Africa to work on the sugar plantations. Many of these new arrivals were strong and courageous. They dreamed of freedom, their hearts filled with the hope of a world where no one was a slave.

Some of the African Groups Taken to Haiti

- The Yoruba People (from West Africa – Nigeria)

  The Yoruba were skilled farmers and traders who valued strong families and tight-knit communities.

- ◈ The Igbo People (from West Africa – Nigeria)

  The Igbo were known for their strength and independence.

- ◈ The Akan People (from West Africa – Ghana and Ivory Coast).

  The Akan were great farmers, warriors, and skilled artisans, especially in pottery-making.

- ◈ The Mandinka People (from West Africa – Senegal and Gambia)

  The Mandinka were fearless warriors, known for their courage and leadership.

- ◈ The Fon People (from West Africa – Benin)

  The Fon were famous for their powerful female warriors, known as the Amazons women who were strong and fierce fighters.

How Did the African Heroes Help Haiti?

The African enslaved people brought to Haiti never gave up. They used their courage, traditions, and strength to fight for their freedom. They worked together, supporting one another, and through their teamwork, they won the Haitian Revolution making Haiti the first country to free enslaved people and gain independence!

These brave men and women from different African tribes like the Yoruba, Igbo, and Akan helped build the Haiti we know today. Their story teaches us that even in the hardest times, when people stand united, they can fight back, stay strong, and create a better future.

What Can We Learn From These Heroes?

- ◈ Never give up – Even when things are tough, keep fighting for what is right.
- ◈ Work together – When people unite, they can achieve amazing things.
- ◈ Be proud of who you are – No matter where you are, your culture and traditions stay with you.

A Divided Island

Haiti shares the island with another colony Santo Domingo, now called the Dominican Republic. Though they spoke different languages and had different ways of life, they were part of the same land, caught between French and Spanish control.

The Rise of a Hero: Toussaint Louverture

Toussaint Louverture was born around 1743 on the Bréda plantation, near Haute du Cap in northern Saint-Domingue (now Haiti). Even though he was enslaved, Toussaint was very intelligent and eager to learn. He taught himself to read and write, which was rare for enslaved people since most were forbidden to go to school.

Toussaint studied military strategy, and some say he even read books on war tactics. This knowledge helped him become a great leader in the fight for freedom.

Jean-Jacques Dessalines: The First Emperor of Haiti

Jean-Jacques Dessalines was born in 1758 in Grande-Rivière-du-Nord, a town in northern Haiti.

After Toussaint Louverture was captured, Jean-Jacques took over the fight for freedom. He led the Haitian army to victory in many battles and became Haiti's first emperor.

He worked hard to make sure Haiti remained free and made certain that no one would ever be enslaved again in his country. He is remembered as a true hero who helped Haiti become the first Black republic in the world.

Mackandal: The Spiritual Leader

François Mackandal was born around 1700 in Senegal, Africa. As a young man, he was taken from his homeland and brought to Haiti, where he was enslaved.

But Mackandal was brave and strong-willed. He escaped from slavery and led groups of runaway slaves who also wanted to be free.

Mackandal was a wise man who knew a lot about medicine and natural remedies. He taught others how to use plants for healing and how to protect themselves. He also became known for using spiritual and mystical knowledge to inspire his people.

His name became legendary because he led many enslaved people in their fight for freedom. His resistance efforts helped inspire the Haitian Revolution, the great fight that finally brought freedom to Haiti.

Boukman: The Brave Leader

Boukman was believed to be from Africa, but some think he might have come from Jamaica instead. Here's why:

From Africa

Some stories say Boukman was taken from Africa and sold into slavery. He was brought to Saint-Domingue, which is now called Haiti.

From Jamaica

Other stories suggest that Boukman was born in Jamaica before being sent to Haiti. At the time, many enslaved people in Jamaica were taken to different parts of the Caribbean.

The truth is, no one knows for sure where Boukman came from because there are no clear records of his early life.

A Leader in the Fight for Freedom

Boukman was an enslaved Jamaican, which meant he had no freedom and was forced to work hard. But he was different from many others. He was smart, strong, and passionate about freedom.

Boukman became a maroon, a person who escaped from slavery and lived in the mountains with others who had run away. These groups of people fought against their captors and tried to live freely.

Boukman's Prayer for Freedom

"God of the sky, we call upon you.
We have suffered under the hands of the French for too long. We are not your slaves. We are human, just like you. Our blood is the same, and our hearts burn with the desire to be free.

Give us strength, courage, and wisdom.
Let the winds of freedom blow through our land.
Let our hearts burn with the fire of justice.
We will fight for our freedom and for the future of our children.
We will not bow to our oppressors.
We will not forget the pain of our ancestors.
We will not let the chains of slavery hold us any longer.
We are one people, one spirit.
Together, we will rise. Together, we will be free.
If we fall, our spirits will live on in the hearts of those who fight. We call upon our ancestors to guide us. Lead us in this battle for freedom.
Lead us to victory.
The time has come. We will break these chains, and we will be free forever.
Amen."

The Fight For Freedom

In 1791, the enslaved people of Haiti rose up against the French, demanding their freedom. They fought bravely under the leadership of Toussaint Louverture. More than 100,000 men, women, and children joined the fight for liberty.

Toussaint's army, made up of former enslaved people, became a powerful force. They fought with strength and determination, defeating the French forces again and again.

The Battle of Vertières

One of the most important battles in the Haitian Revolution was the Battle of Vertières, fought on November 18, 1803.

The battle was led by Jean-Jacques Dessalines, a strong and fearless leader. He organized an army called the Indigenous Army. Though they were not Native Americans, they called themselves this because they were the true people of Haiti, fighting to take back their land from the French.

Most of Dessalines' soldiers were formerly enslaved people who had been forced to work on plantations. Now, they were warriors fighting for their freedom.

The French Army and the Final Victory

The French army was led by General Charles Leclerc, who had been sent by Napoleon Bonaparte, the ruler of France. The French had a strong army with powerful weapons, ships, and thousands of soldiers.

But the Haitian people would not give up. They fought bravely, using their knowledge of the land to their advantage. After many hours of fierce battle, the Haitian army won!

This victory led to Haiti becoming the first country in the world to gain freedom from slavery and colonial rule.

Haiti's fight for independence inspired enslaved people all over the world. Boukman, Toussaint Louverture, and Jean-Jacques Dessalines helped change history, proving that freedom is worth fighting for.

1. **A Leader**

    The French army was led by a man named Napoleon Bonaparte. He was known for winning many battles and was a brilliant strategist. People thought he was one of the greatest army leaders in the world because he knew how to train his soldiers and lead them to victory.

2. **Great Training**

    The soldiers in the French army were trained very well. They practiced a lot and learned different ways to fight, making them strong and prepared for battle. This helped them win many wars.

3. **A Big and Powerful Navy**

    The French also had a powerful navy a fleet of large ships that could sail across the oceans. These ships helped France protect its colonies and trade with other countries.

Even though the French army was strong, they could not win in Haiti. The Haitian people, led by brave leaders like Jean-Jacques Dessalines, were determined to fight for their freedom.

The French tried many times to take control of Haiti, but the Haitian fighters never gave up. They were fearless and kept fighting until they won their independence.

The Day of the Battle

On the day of the battle, Jean-Jacques Dessalines and his soldiers were ready to fight the French in a place called Vertières, near the city of Cap-

Français (now known as Cap-Haïtien). The Haitian fighters were mostly former enslaved people, and they wanted one thing freedom.

The French army was well-trained and had many weapons, but they had been fighting for a long time and were tired. Even though the Haitian soldiers had fewer weapons and were outnumbered, they fought with all their strength. They believed in their cause and had powerful leaders to guide them one of the bravest was Capois La Mort.

Who Was Capois La Mort?

Capois La Mort was one of Haiti's greatest heroes. His name means "Captain Death" because he was so fearless in battle. He was known for his incredible bravery and never gave up, no matter how difficult the fight became.

The Famous Moment

During the Battle of Vertières, Capois La Mort showed unbelievable courage. At one point, a bullet hit his horse, and the horse fell to the ground. But Capois jumped up, grabbed his sword, and kept fighting on foot. He called out to his soldiers:

"They will have to kill me before I give up!"

His bravery inspired the Haitian fighters to keep going.

One of the most famous moments of the battle happened when Capois saw a French cannon. The French had set up huge cannons to stop the Haitians. But Capois wasn't afraid! He ran straight toward the cannon and, with a loud, fearless voice, shouted:

"Forward, my brave soldiers, forward!"

Even though he was in great danger, he kept fighting. His courage helped the Haitians win the battle.

The Victory

By the end of the day, the Haitian soldiers had won. The French had lost, and they realized they could no longer control Haiti.

This battle was the final fight of the Haitian Revolution. Soon after, Haiti became an independent country, and it became the first nation in the world to completely abolish slavery.

The Polish Heroes

Some Polish soldiers came to Haiti because they were working for the French army. These soldiers didn't choose to be in the war they were forced to fight for France.

But when they arrived in Haiti, they saw something that changed everything. The Haitian people were fighting for their freedom, just like the Polish people wanted for their own country, which was not independent at the time.

Some Polish soldiers decided they didn't want to fight for the French anymore. Instead, they joined the Haitians and helped them in their battle for freedom. Together, the Polish and Haitian fighters worked side by side to defeat the French.

When Haiti became free in 1804, the Polish soldiers who had helped were given land and homes in Haiti as a reward for their bravery. Some of them stayed in Haiti, while others returned to Europe. Their story shows that people from different places can come together to fight for freedom.

The Courage of the Women

Aunt Toya: The Warrior Who Raised a Hero

Aunt Toya was a special woman in the life of Jean-Jacques Dessalines, one of Haiti's greatest heroes. She was like a second mother to him she took care of him, taught him, and helped him grow into a strong and brave leader.

But Aunt Toya wasn't just kind and wise she was also a fierce warrior! She was a general in the famous all-woman army called the Amazons from the Kingdom of Dahomey (now Benin). These warriors were known for their incredible strength, skill, and bravery on the battlefield.

Aunt Toya didn't just fight she was a smart warrior. She passed her knowledge to Dessalines, teaching him how to lead his people to victory.

What Aunt Toya Taught Dessalines

- **Battle Strategies** – Fighting wasn't just about being strong. Aunt Toya taught Dessalines how to plan ahead and outthink the enemy.
- **Using the Land** – She showed him how to use the environment, like mountains and forests, to stay hidden and surprise the enemy.
- **Bravery and Teamwork** – Aunt Toya taught that warriors don't fight alone they work together to win.
- **The Power of Surprise** – The Amazon warriors were known for sneaky and smart attacks. She taught Dessalines how to catch the enemy off guard.
- **Fighting for Freedom** – She made sure Dessalines understood that the most important reason to fight was for freedom.
- **Strength and Discipline** – Being a warrior wasn't just about battle. Aunt Toya taught self-control, discipline, and focus, which made Dessalines a great leader.

Because of Aunt Toya's training, Dessalines became a fierce and intelligent leader. Her teachings helped him lead Haiti to freedom, using both strength and wisdom.

1. **Cécile Fatiman:** The Woman Who Sparked a Revolution

Who Was Cécile Fatiman?

Cécile Fatiman was a strong and wise woman who played a major role in the Haitian Revolution. She was known for her deep connection to Vodou, an important spiritual tradition in Haitian culture.

How Did She Help?

Cécile Fatiman was a leader in a secret meeting called the Bois Caïman Ceremony in 1791. At this gathering, enslaved people came together and promised to fight for their freedom.

Cécile led a powerful spiritual ceremony that gave the people courage and determination to begin the revolution. Her leadership inspired the fighters to start a rebellion that eventually led to Haiti becoming the first country to free itself from slavery!

2. **Sanite Belair**

Who Was She?

Sanite Belair was a brave woman who married Charles Bélair, a hero of the Haitian Revolution. Born into slavery, she refused to accept a life without freedom. Sanité was strong, smart, and determined to see Haiti free.

How Did She Help?

When her husband died in battle, Sanité didn't give up. She picked up a sword and kept fighting for Haiti's independence. As a leader, she planned attacks, commanded soldiers, and inspired those around her. Sadly, she was captured and executed, but her courage made her a symbol of resistance. Today, she is remembered as a hero who never stopped fighting for freedom.

3. Marie-Jeanne Lamartinière

Who Was She?

Marie-Jeanne Lamartinière was born into slavery, but she had a fearless spirit and believed everyone deserved to be free. She was determined to fight for her rights and the rights of others.

How Did She Help?

Marie-Jeanne joined the revolution and fought in many battles. She didn't stay on the sidelines she fought with strength and bravery. One of the most important battles she took part in was the Battle of Vertières in 1803, where the Haitian army defeated the French. She proved that women were just as strong and courageous as men in the fight for freedom.

4. Madeleine L'Ouverture

Who Was She?

Madeleine L'Ouverture was the daughter of Toussaint L'Ouverture, one of Haiti's most famous leaders. Her father, often called the "Black Napoleon," led the Haitian people in their fight for independence.

How Did She Help?

Unlike her father, Madeleine wasn't a warrior, but she played an important role in the revolution. She supported the fight for freedom by spreading messages of justice and standing by her father and the Haitian revolutionaries. Her actions showed that every family member mothers, fathers, daughters, and sons had a role in Haiti's fight for independence.

5. Madan Létan: The Mysterious and Resilient Spirit

Who Was She?

Madan Létan is remembered as a powerful and mysterious woman from the time of the Haitian Revolution. Some believe she was involved in spiritual and religious ceremonies, while others say she was a Vodou leader who inspired people to fight for their freedom.

How Did She Help?

During the revolution, many Haitians turned to their cultural beliefs, like Vodou, for strength. Madan Létan was said to be part of this community, guiding and uniting people in their struggle. Though details of her life remain unclear, many believe her wisdom and connection to the spirits of nature gave people hope. She symbolized the resilience and strength of the Haitian people.

6. Lovana: A Symbol of Resistance

Who Was She?

Lovana was an important figure in Haiti's fight against oppression. While there isn't much written about her, she represents the many women who fought alongside men to resist colonization.

How Did She Help?

Lovana's story is a reminder that women played powerful roles behind the scenes. She and others like her helped strengthen the revolution by spreading messages of unity, supporting fighters, and sometimes even joining battles. Though not as well-known as some leaders, Lovana stands as a symbol of Haitian women's courage and determination.

These two women, Madan Létan and Lovana, represent the many unsung heroes of Haiti's history. Their stories prove that everyone no matter their gender played a vital role in Haiti's struggle for freedom.

7. **Adélaïde**

Who Was She?

Adélaïde was an enslaved woman who escaped and joined the maroon communities groups of runaway slaves who built their own villages and fought back against their captors.

How Did She Help?

Clever and fearless, Adélaïde helped organize revolts and attacks against French and Spanish soldiers. Using her knowledge of the land, she and her fellow maroons outsmarted the enemy. Though she wasn't a famous general, her actions played a key role in Haiti's fight for independence.

Why Are These Women Heroes?

These women were not just warriors they were leaders, thinkers, and symbols of strength. They helped change the history of Haiti and the world. Because of their courage, Haiti became the first country to break free from slavery, and their stories continue to inspire people everywhere. Their actions remind us that anyone, no matter who they are, can make a difference in the fight for freedom and justice.

The End of Slavery

In 1804, after a long and bloody struggle, Haiti declared its independence. Jean-Jacques Dessalines, one of the great leaders of the revolution, became the first emperor of Haiti. He signed the Declaration of Independence, marking a historic moment.

Haiti became the first independent nation in Latin America and the Caribbean. It was also the first country where enslaved people fought back, won their freedom, and created a new nation where everyone, no matter their skin color, was free.

The Spirit Lives On

Today, the spirit of the Taino people and the revolution's heroes Toussaint Louverture, Dessalines, Cécile Fatiman, and even the brave Polish soldiers still live on in the hearts of the Haitian people. Haiti's history teaches us that even in the darkest times, there is always hope, and no one should ever stop fighting for their freedom.

A New Tomorrow

Haiti's story is one of bravery, unity, and triumph. The people of Haiti continue to honor their past, carrying the flame of independence and freedom for all. This story celebrates Haiti's incredible journey from the time of the Taino people, through the struggles and victories of the Haitian Revolution, to the birth of a free nation. It is a tale of heroes from all walks of life, showing that with courage and unity, anything is possible.

A Beacon of Freedom

After Haiti won its independence in 1804, it became the first country in the world where enslaved people fought for and won their freedom. Haiti's fight for equality became an inspiration for other nations, especially in Latin America, where many countries were still ruled by European powers.

Haiti's victory showed that it was possible to resist and win, even against powerful enemies. Many Latin American countries wanted to follow Haiti's example and free themselves from European rule, and they turned to Haiti for help.

How Haiti Helped Other Countries Gain Their Independence

On January 1, 1804, Haiti became an independent country after defeating the French, who had controlled it for many years. This was a historic moment because Haiti became the first country where enslaved people fought for their freedom and won.

Haiti's Act of Independence was like an official letter that declared, "*We are free now!*" It was written by Boisrond-Tonnerre, who helped put into words why Haiti was breaking away from France. Jean-Jacques Dessalines, one of Haiti's revolutionary leaders, read the declaration aloud in the city of Gonaïves.

This document not only announced Haiti's freedom but also promised that slavery would never exist there again. Haiti became the first country in the world to completely abolish slavery a huge moment in the fight for human rights!

But Haiti's fight for freedom didn't stop there. After gaining its independence, Haiti helped other countries in their struggles for freedom too. It sent soldiers, weapons, and money to support independence movements in countries like Mexico, Venezuela, and the Dominican Republic.

Let's look at some of the countries Haiti helped and the heroes from those countries who became famous for their own independence struggles:

8. **Venezuela**

In Venezuela, there was a great hero named Simón Bolívar, also known as the *"Liberator."* Bolívar dreamed of a free Latin America, but he needed help to win his battles.

That's when Haitian President Alexandre Pétion stepped in. Pétion believed that all people deserved to be free, so he gave Bolívar money, weapons, and even soldiers to help him fight.

With Haiti's support, Bolívar was able to continue his mission and eventually freed several countries in Latin America from Spanish rule.

9. **The Dominican Republic**

The Dominican Republic shares the island of Hispaniola with Haiti. In the early 1800s, the country was under French rule, and its people wanted freedom too.

When the Dominican Republic fought for independence from Spain, Haitian leader Jean-Pierre Boyer sent troops to help the rebels. Without Haiti's support, the Dominican Republic might not have been able to break free.

Even though Haiti and the Dominican Republic later had disagreements, Haiti's help in the country's early struggles for independence was very important.

10. **Mexico**

In Mexico, leaders like Agustín de Iturbide fought to gain independence from Spain. During Mexico's fight for freedom, Haitian President Alexandre Pétion once again stepped up to help.

He sent soldiers, money, and weapons to support the Mexican fighters. These contributions played a big role in helping Mexico finally win its independence from Spain in 1821.

Why Did Haiti Help Other Countries?

Haiti's leaders wanted to spread the message that everyone deserves to be free.

They had fought so hard to win their own freedom, and they didn't want other people to suffer under the rule of slave masters. By helping other countries, Haiti became a symbol of hope for freedom and justice.

The Haitian Heroes Who Helped

Here are some of the Haitian leaders who played an important role in helping other countries gain independence:

- **Alexandre Pétion** – As President of Haiti, Pétion sent support to leaders like Simón Bolívar in Venezuela and Agustín de Iturbide in Mexico. He provided resources and even sent Haitian soldiers to fight for freedom. He believed that the independence of all nations was important.
- **Jean-Pierre Boyer** – Boyer helped the Dominican Republic by sending Haitian troops to support their fight against Spain. Under his leadership, the Haitian government continued to assist other countries in their struggles for independence.
- **Toussaint Louverture** – Although Toussaint Louverture did not fight directly in other countries' independence movements, his leadership and courage inspired freedom fighters across the world. Many leaders, including Simón Bolívar, saw Louverture as proof that enslaved people could rise up and win their freedom.

The Bigger Picture: Freedom Spreads

Thanks to Haiti's help, many countries in Latin America and the Caribbean gained their freedom and became independent nations.

Haiti's bravery and determination proved to the world that oppressed people could fight back and win. The Haitian heroes who helped other countries became symbols of hope and freedom, and their stories are still celebrated today.

The Important Lesson from Haiti's Help

Haiti's story teaches us the power of unity and helping others.

Even though Haiti had its own struggles, it didn't turn its back on other nations that needed help. Instead, Haiti shared its strength and resources to help them achieve their own freedom.

This reminds us that when we fight for justice and freedom, it's important to help others who are struggling too. Together, we can build a better, fairer world for everyone.

The Haitian Flag

History of the Flag

The Haitian flag was first created on May 18, 1803. A woman named Catherine Flon helped make it. She took the French flag, which had three colors blue, white, and red and removed the white part. Then, she sewed the blue and red together to create a new flag for Haiti!

Why the Colors Are Important:

- Blue represents the formerly enslaved Black people who fought for freedom.
- Red represents the mulattoes people with both African and European ancestry.

By joining blue and red together, the flag symbolized that all Haitians, no matter their background, were united in their fight for freedom from the French.

The Flag's Meaning Today

The Haitian flag is more than just a symbol it represents the freedom and unity of the Haitian people. It reminds everyone of how they fought together to create their own nation. Every year, on May 18, Haitians celebrate Flag Day to honor the day their flag was created.

So, the Haitian flag isn't just about colors it's a powerful reminder of the bravery and determination of the Haitian people!

Symbolism in the Flag

In the center of the flag, you often see a palm tree, cannons, and cannonballs. These symbols represent:

- The fight for freedom
- The strength of the Haitian people

Haitian Folklore and Religion

Vodou

One of the most well-known parts of Haitian culture is Vodou. This religion blends African spiritual beliefs with Christianity. In Vodou, people believe in spirits called Loa, and the religion is deeply connected to everyday life in Haiti.

Folktales

Haiti has many folk stories about clever characters who teach important life lessons. Two famous characters are:

- **Bouki** – A foolish but lovable character.
- **Timalice** – A smart and tricky character who always finds a way to win!

These stories have been passed down for generations and continue to teach lessons about wisdom, cleverness, and life.

Agriculture in Haiti

What Haiti Grows

Haiti has rich, fertile land where many different crops grow. The country is known for producing some of the best coffee beans in the world. It also grows cacao, which is used to make chocolate. Other important crops include sugarcane, mangoes, bananas, and cocoa.

Haitian Society and Unity

A Diverse Population

Haiti is home to people from different backgrounds. Many Haitians are descendants of African Taino, while others have French and Spanish heritage. Haitian culture values strong family bonds and close-knit communities.

Unity

Haitians take great pride in their country's fight for freedom. The Haitian Revolution is a powerful example of how people can overcome challenges when they work together. This spirit of unity is still an important part of Haitian culture today.

Haitian Sports

Soccer (Football)

Soccer is the most popular sport in Haiti. The Haitian national team has performed well in international competitions and even qualified for the FIFA World Cup in 1974!

Other Sports

Besides soccer, Haitians also enjoy basketball, volleyball, and boxing. These sports reflect Haiti's strong traditions of teamwork and community.

Haiti's Influence on Other Caribbean Countries

Symbol of Freedom

When Haiti won independence from France in 1804, it became an inspiration for other Caribbean and Latin American nations. Leaders like Simón Bolívar of Venezuela were influenced by Haiti's struggle for freedom.

Cultural Influence

Haitian culture has spread across the Caribbean, especially through music, dance, and the Vodou religion.

Haitian Music

Konpa and Rara

Haiti is famous for its lively music. Konpa has a smooth, rhythmic beat, while Rara is played during festivals and celebrations. Both styles bring people together in joy and dance.

Influence on the World

Haitian music has influenced many other genres, including jazz, reggae, and salsa. Some Haitian musicians have even gained international fame!

Haitian Dance

Rara Dance

Rara is a traditional Haitian dance performed at festivals. It features lively drumming, singing, and energetic movements, creating a fun and exciting atmosphere.

Other Dance Styles

Haitian dance also includes Bendò, a popular social dance, and Meringue, which is enjoyed throughout the Caribbean.

Haitian Art

A World of Color

Haitian artists are known for their bright, colorful paintings that show everyday life, nature, and Haitian culture. Art is a big part of life in Haiti, and many Haitian artists have become famous around the world.

The Haitian Art Movement

The Haitian art movement began in the mid-20th century. It is known for its bold colors and unique style, often inspired by history and religion.

The Influence of Haiti on Art

Haitian Art on the Global Stage

Haitian art has influenced artists everywhere. Famous Haitian artists like Philippe Dodard and Préfète Duffaut have displayed their work in international galleries, helping to share Haiti's beauty and culture with the world.

Haitian Cuisine

What Haitians Eat

Haitian food is full of flavor and spice! Popular dishes include griot (fried pork), rice and beans, and pikliz (spicy cabbage salad). Haitians also enjoy plantains, cornmeal dishes, and soup joumou a special pumpkin soup eaten on Independence Day.

Haitian Festivals and Celebrations

Carnival

Haiti celebrates Carnival, a huge festival filled with music, dancing, and parades. It is a joyful time that happens before Lent.

Independence Day

On January 1st, Haitians celebrate Independence Day to remember when they became free from French rule in 1804. This day is very important in Haitian history!

Haiti's National Symbols

Haiti National Anthem name is "La Dessalinnienne" written by Justin L'herisson and composed by Nicolas Geffrard

Haitian National Bird: The Hispaniolan Trogon

Haiti's national bird is the Hispaniolan Trogon. This colorful bird is special because it only lives on the island of Hispaniola, which is home to Haiti and the Dominican Republic. The trogon represents Haiti's uniqueness just like this rare bird, Haiti is one of a kind!

Haitian National Flower: The Hibiscus

Haiti's national flowers of Haiti the Hibiscus Flower .This bright and beautiful flower is a symbol of Haiti's strength and lively spirit. People all over the country grow hibiscus in their gardens. Its bold red and pink petals remind Haitians of their vibrant culture.

The Tallest Mountain in Haiti: Pic la Selle

Haiti is home to many mountains, but the tallest one is Pic la Selle. It reaches 8,793 feet (2,680 meters) high so tall it seems to touch the sky! This mountain is near the town of Côte de Fer and is part of the Chaîne de la Selle mountain range.

Pic la Selle is not just tall it is also home to rare plants and animals. Hikers love climbing this mountain to see the amazing views from the top.

Haiti's 10 Departments:

Haiti is split into 10 parts called *"departments,"* like how a big country might be split into states or provinces. Each department is different from the others in terms of what it looks like and what it grows. Here's a little about each department:

- **Artibonite** – This department is like the farming heart of Haiti! It grows a lot of rice. Artibonite has big fields with water, where rice can grow well, and it's one of the most important crops in Haiti.
- **Centre** – Centre is full of mountains and valleys. People here grow beans and corn. These foods are really important for feeding families all over Haiti.
- **Grand'Anse** – Grand'Anse is known for its pretty beaches and warm weather. It grows bananas and coconuts. These are tropical fruits that people love to eat, and they're found all along the coast.
- **Nippes** – Nippes is a smaller department, but it's famous for growing cassava (a type of root vegetable) and coconut. Cassava is used in many Haitian dishes.
- **North** – The North is home to some of Haiti's most famous history, like the Citadelle Laferrière, a huge fort. The people there grow coffee and cocoa, which are used to make delicious drinks and chocolate!

- **Northeast** – The Northeast is a place where lots of crops grow, like rice, corn, and beans. It's a great place for farming because of the fertile land and many rivers that help water the crops.
- **West** – The West is where the capital, Port-au-Prince, is located. It's a busy area with a lot of people. In the West, people grow citrus fruits (like oranges), sugarcane, and coffee. These crops are important to Haiti's economy.
- **South** – The South has beautiful beaches and historic towns like Jacmel. People grow coffee, bananas, and sugarcane. The warm weather makes it perfect for tropical crops.
- **Southeast** – The Southeast is a mountainous area, with lots of rivers and forests. People there grow citrus fruits, cassava, and plantains (a type of banana). The land is good for farming.
- **La Gonâve** – La Gonâve is a small island, and people there grow coconuts and other crops like cassava. It's peaceful, and the island is surrounded by the sea, so it's also known for fishing.

Do any of these things about Haiti spark your curiosity?

Haitian History and Important Events

January 1, 1804 – Haiti's Independence Day

What happened?

On January 1, 1804, Haiti became the first country in the world where enslaved people fought for their freedom and won! This historic victory ended slavery in Haiti and made it a free nation. Two important leaders, Jean-Jacques Dessalines and Toussaint Louverture, led many battles to defeat the French, who wanted to keep Haiti as a colony. This is why January 1st is such an important day for Haitians it marks their freedom!

- Why is it special?

This day represents Haiti's independence and proves that people can fight for their freedom, no matter how difficult the struggle.

May 18, 1805 – Haiti's Flag Day

- What happened?

On this day, Haiti officially created its national flag! The flag has two colors blue and red each with special meaning. The blue represents Black Haitians, and the red represents people of mixed race. The flag was designed to show that everyone, no matter their background, is an important part of the country.

- Why is it special?

Haiti's flag is a powerful symbol of unity and pride. It reminds Haitians of their strength and the fight for a free nation.

August 14, 1791 – The Bois Caïman Ceremony (The Beginning of the Haitian Revolution)

On this day, a group of brave people secretly gathered in the woods to plan their fight for freedom. They wanted to end slavery and stop the bad treatment from the French slave masters.

The meeting was led by important leaders who believed in both fighting for freedom and asking for spiritual help. During this ceremony:

- They performed a ritual, which is like a special prayer or ceremony to ask for strength.
- As part of the ritual, they sacrificed a pig, which was a way to show their commitment.
- They promised to fight together until they were free.

The Bois Caïman ceremony is remembered because it was the moment when people joined forces to start the Haitian Revolution a fight that led to freedom and equality!

November 18, 1803 – The Battle of Vertières

In 1803, the Haitian army, made up of brave soldiers and former enslaved people, fought the French in an important battle called the Battle of Vertières. This was one of the last battles of the Haitian Revolution.

Why is this battle important?

- The Haitians won, forcing the French to leave Haiti.
- It was a huge victory that led to Haiti's independence.
- It showed the strength and courage of the Haitian people!

The Battle of Vertières is remembered as one of the greatest victories for freedom in history!

The Battle of Vertières

- Date: November 18, 1803
- Where it happened: Near Vertières, a town in northern Haiti, close to Cap-Haïtien.

What Happened During the Battle of Vertières?

In 1803, Haiti was still fighting against the French army, which was trying to take back control of the island. The Haitian soldiers, mostly former enslaved people, had joined the fight for freedom. They were led by Jean-Jacques Dessalines and other brave leaders.

During the battle, the Haitian soldiers faced the French army, which had better weapons and more soldiers. Even though the Haitians were outnumbered, they never gave up! They fought with courage and determination because they wanted to be free from slavery and French rule.

The Haitian army won the battle! This victory was a huge moment in history because it showed the world that the Haitian people were strong and determined to fight for their freedom. After this battle, the French soldiers realized they couldn't win and soon left Haiti for good.

Why Is the Battle of Vertières Important?

- It helped Haiti win its independence!

After the victory, Haiti was almost completely free from French rule. Just a few months later, on January 1, 1804, Haiti became the first independent nation in Latin America and the Caribbean.

- It was a victory for freedom!

The battle showed that even though Haiti had suffered a long history of slavery, the people fought for their rights and won their freedom.

- Haitians proved their strength and bravery!

The battle is a symbol of courage, reminding people that fighting for what's right can lead to great victories.

Rivers, and Waterfalls in Haiti

Haiti is full of beautiful water sources, and there are many rivers and waterfalls that make the country unique. Let's take a look!

1. **Rivers in Haiti**

   - Artibonite River: This is the longest river in Haiti. It's very important because it helps water many of the crops that people grow in Haiti, like rice.
   - Rivière Grise: This river flows through the capital city of Haiti, Port-au-Prince. It's an important part of the city's daily life.
   - Rivière du Nord: This river is in the north of Haiti and also helps many people with farming and getting water for daily use.

2. **Waterfalls in Haiti**

   - Saut-d'Eau Waterfall: This waterfall is very famous in Haiti. It's a beautiful waterfall located near a town called Saut-d'Eau. People often visit it to enjoy the view, and it also has religious importance because some people believe the water from the waterfall has special healing powers.
   - Bassin-Bleu: This is another very beautiful spot in Haiti. It has blue water and waterfalls that people love to visit to swim and enjoy nature.
   - Bassin Caiman: This waterfall is like a secret hidden in the forest, far away from busy places. It's surrounded by trees and nature, so you feel like you're in a magical jungle. It's perfect for people who like to explore quiet, beautiful places.
   - Cascade de Pichon: This one is near a town called Pétion-Ville. It's a lovely waterfall where you can hike up to see the water falling down and swim in the cool, fresh water below.

So, if you like the sound of waterfalls and cool adventures, Haiti has some awesome spots for you to visit!

Varieties of Mangoes in Haiti

Haiti is famous for its mangoes, and there are many types that people love to eat! Here are a few of them:

- **Mango Francique:** This mango is sweet and juicy, and it's one of the most common types in Haiti. It has a smooth texture and is loved by many people.

- **Mango Jean Marie:** This mango is smaller than the others but is very sweet. It's soft and delicious, and people really enjoy it!
- **Mango Rosalie:** This mango tastes a little like pineapple, with a tangy flavor, but still very sweet. It's a little different from the others, which makes it special.
- **Mango Baptiste:** This mango is bigger and has a firmer texture. It's less sweet than other types, but still a great mango!

These mangoes are grown in different parts of Haiti and are loved by people all over the country. Haiti's warm climate makes it perfect for growing lots of different fruits, especially mangoes!

Important Haitian Monuments and Forts

Haiti has many important monuments that show the strength, history, and beauty of the country. Some of the most famous ones are:

Citadelle Laferrière (The Citadel)

- What is it? The Citadelle Laferrière is a giant fortress built on a mountain in northern Haiti. It was built by King Henri Christophe after Haiti became independent. He wanted to make sure that Haiti was protected from any enemies, especially the French, who might try to take over again.
- Why is it important? It is one of the strongest and most famous forts in the world! It shows how hard the Haitian people fought for their freedom. The Citadel is also a UNESCO World Heritage Site, which means it is considered one of the most special places in the world.

Fort de la Ferrière (Another Fort by Dessalines)

- What is it? Jean-Jacques Dessalines, one of Haiti's most famous leaders, helped build the Fort de la Ferrière as a defense against foreign attacks. It was part of the larger Citadelle complex.
- Palais de Belle-Vue in Limonade is a special place in Haiti, like an old castle that was built a long time ago. A king named Henri Christophe who was an important leader during Haiti's fight for freedom built

this palace to show how powerful he was after Haiti became free from France.

- Why is it important? The fort was a symbol of freedom and strength, built to protect the people of Haiti and show that they wouldn't be conquered again.

The Statue of Jean-Jacques Dessalines

- What is it? There's a statue of Jean-Jacques Dessalines in the capital city, Port-au-Prince, to honor him as one of Haiti's greatest leaders.
- Why is it important? Dessalines was a hero in the Haitian Revolution, and the statue continues to remind people of how much he helped Haiti gain freedom.

Treats from Haiti!

Haitian sweets are full of fun flavors! Here are some tasty ones:

- **Bonbon Sirop** – These tiny, chewy candies Crackers made with honey and flour tale out the coconut and pineapple. They're sweet and fun to snack on!
- **Bonbon Lanmidon** – Soft and colorful, these squishy Crackers are made from cornstarch and sugar. They taste good and melt in your mouth!
- **Cassave** – A crispy cracker-like snack made from cassava, a tropical plant. It's super crunchy and great for munching!
- **Mamba** – A smooth and creamy Haitian peanut butter. You can spread it on bread, crackers, or even eat it straight from the spoon delicious!

So, whether you want something chewy, crunchy, or creamy, Haitian kids have lots of fun snacks to enjoy!

Haiti's Soccer Team and the World Cup

Haiti has a soccer team, just like many other countries! In 1974, the team worked really hard, playing many games to earn a spot in the biggest soccer tournament in the world the World Cup! It was an exciting moment for Haiti, showing their talent and determination on the world stage.

Tasty Haitian Snacks!

Haitian kids love delicious snacks, and here are some of their favorites:

Marinad

Marinad is a crunchy, golden-brown fried dough snack. It's crispy on the outside and soft inside. Made with flour, salt, and sometimes tasty spices or herbs, it's perfect for munching when you're hungry. Imagine little, crispy dough balls that melt in your mouth yum!

Akra

Akra is another yummy fried snack, but it's made with malanga, a root vegetable that looks like a potato. The malanga is grated, mixed with flour and spices, then fried until golden and crispy. It's crunchy on the outside, soft inside, and often enjoyed with a spicy dipping sauce. So good!

Haitian kids enjoy these snacks after school, at parties, or anytime they're craving something delicious. They're perfect for sharing with friends!

Languages in Haiti

In Haiti, people speak two main languages: Haitian Creole and French.

- Haitian Creole *("Kreyòl Ayisyen")*

Most people in Haiti speak Haitian Creole every day! This special language was created by mixing African languages with French. It's important because it connects Haitians to their history. Creole is also full of fun sayings and proverbs short, wise sentences that teach lessons or make people laugh!

- French

French is used in schools, government, and official places, but most Haitians speak Creole at home and in everyday life. Creole is also a symbol of Haiti's independence because it was the language of the people who fought to free Haiti from slavery.

Music and Dance in Haiti

Music is a huge part of Haitian life! It's what makes Haiti special, bringing people together to celebrate, tell stories, and express emotions. Here are some popular types of music in Haiti:

- **Konpa:** The most famous style of music in Haiti! It has smooth, slow beats that make you want to dance. Konpa is often played at parties, weddings, and celebrations, where people dance with fun, flowing movements.
- **Rara:** A special type of music played during Carnival and other celebrations. It's full of drums, horns, and maracas, creating a loud, energetic sound. Rara bands march through the streets, playing music and singing together!
- **Mizik Rasin (Roots Music):** This music tells the history of Haiti. It mixes traditional Haitian rhythms with rock and jazz, creating powerful songs about freedom and unity.

In Haiti, music isn't just for fun it tells stories! Dancing is also important. Whether it's a slow dance to compas or a fast, joyful dance to rara, Haitians love to express themselves through movement!

Art in Haiti

Haitian art is bright, colorful, and full of life! When you look at Haitian art, you'll see bold colors, strong shapes, and creative designs. Many artists paint pictures of daily life, nature, and important moments in Haiti's history.

- **Haitian Paintings:** Haitian paintings are famous around the world! They use bright colors to show people working, playing music, or celebrating life.
- **Vodou Art:** Vodou is a Haitian religion, and its art is full of symbols and powerful images. People paint and sculpt spirits and gods, creating artwork that has deep meaning.
- **Metal Art:** Some Haitian artists create beautiful sculptures from scrap metal! They turn things like old cans into animals, flowers, and people. These artists take things others throw away and turn them into amazing pieces of art!

Haitian art tells stories, shows culture, and celebrates life in a unique way!

Food in Haiti

Haitian food is full of flavor! It's a mix of African, French, and Native Taino traditions, creating delicious dishes full of spices and fresh ingredients. Here are some of the most popular foods in Haiti:

- **Griot:** Crispy, flavorful fried pork, marinated in spices and served with fried plantains (bananas) and pikliz (a spicy vegetable mix). It's a favorite for parties and gatherings!
- **Soup Joumou:** A special soup made with squash, vegetables, and meat. Haitians eat this soup on New Year's Day as a symbol of freedom. Long ago, enslaved people weren't allowed to eat this soup, but after Haiti gained independence, it became a symbol of victory!
- **Rice and Beans:** A classic Haitian meal! The rice and beans are cooked with spices and meat, making a warm, comforting dish that many families eat every day.

Haitian food is not just about taste it's about family and togetherness! Every meal is a time to share, celebrate, and enjoy life.

Why Do Haitians Make Soup Joumou?

A long time ago, in Haiti, there were enslaved people who worked very hard but were not allowed to eat the delicious Joumou squash. The French people who ruled Haiti said that only they could eat this squash.

But when Haiti became free on January 1, 1804, the people of Haiti celebrated their freedom by cooking and eating Soup Joumou. This was a way to say, *"Now, we're free, and we can eat the same food as everyone else!"*

So every year, on January 1st, Haitians make Soup Joumou to remember how they fought for freedom and to celebrate being a free country!

Ingredients in Soup Joumou

Here's what's usually in Soup Joumou:

- **Joumou (Squash)** – This is the main ingredient! It gives the soup its bright yellow color and creamy texture.
- **Beef** – Small pieces of beef are cooked in the soup for flavor.
- **Carrots** – These are cut up into little pieces and add sweetness and color.
- **Potatoes** – These make the soup feel more filling and tasty.
- **Celery and Leeks** – These add flavor to the soup.
- **Garlic** – These make the soup smell yummy and savory.
- **Spices** – Things like thyme, bay leaves, and a little hot pepper give the soup a wonderful taste.

- **Pasta or Noodles** – Small pasta is often added to make the soup more filling.
- **Lime or Vinegar** – A little bit of lime or vinegar makes the soup taste fresh and zesty.

How to Make Soup Joumou (Easy Steps)

- **Cook the Beef:** First, you cook the beef with some spices to make it really flavorful.
- **Prepare the Squash:** Boil the squash until it's soft, then mash it up to make the soup creamy.
- **Cook the Vegetables:** Chop up the carrots, potatoes, and other veggies, and cook them until they're soft.
- **Combine Everything:** Mix the beef, squash, veggies, and spices in a big pot. Add water to make it soupy.
- **Add Pasta:** If you're using noodles, you can add them in last, so they cook up soft and tasty.
- **Taste and Adjust:** Add salt, pepper, and lime or vinegar to make it taste just right!

Why Is Soup Joumou So Important?

- **It Celebrates Freedom** – Soup Joumou is made every year on January 1st, Haiti's Independence Day. It reminds everyone of the brave fight for freedom. Long ago, Haitian people couldn't eat certain foods, but after gaining independence, they could enjoy whatever they wanted. This soup is a symbol of that victory!
- **A Special Tradition** – Making Soup Joumou is a tradition that brings families together. On Independence Day, Haitian families cook and eat the soup while sharing stories about their history. It's a way to stay connected to the past and celebrate freedom with loved ones.
- **Unity** – No matter where Haitians live, they still make and eat Soup Joumou on January 1st. It's a dish that unites them and helps them remember their roots, even if they're far from home.

So, in short, Soup Joumou is more than just a tasty soup it's a symbol of strength, unity, and pride for the Haitian people! Every year, Haitians celebrate their freedom by making and sharing this delicious squash soup.

Clothing and Fashion

Haitian fashion is vibrant and colorful just like the country itself! People in Haiti often wear bright, patterned clothes that reflect their joyful culture.

- **Traditional Clothing:** Haitians wear colorful skirts, blouses, and dresses, especially during holidays and festivals. Women often wear headscarves, and their outfits are made from beautiful, patterned fabrics.
- **Modern Fashion:** Young Haitians also enjoy wearing modern clothes like jeans, shirts, and dresses. But no matter what, their outfits are always bright and fun, showing the energy and spirit of Haitian culture.

Sports in Haiti

Haitians love sports, and soccer (called football in Haiti) is the most popular one! Kids play soccer everywhere on the streets, in fields, and even on the beach. Haitians take great pride in their national soccer team, and when there's a big game, everyone comes together to cheer for their country.

Besides soccer, Haitians also enjoy basketball, track and field, and boxing. Sports bring people together, allowing them to have fun, show their talents, and celebrate their Haitian pride.

Religion in Haiti

Religion is very important in Haiti. Most Haitians practice Christianity, either Catholicism or Protestantism. Families go to church to pray, sing, and celebrate their faith. Haitian Christians also celebrate special holidays like Christmas and Easter with joyful gatherings.

Another important religion in Haiti is Vodou. Vodou is an African-based religion that blends African traditions with Catholic beliefs. People who practice Vodou believe in spirits that help them in their daily lives. Though often misunderstood, Vodou is a meaningful part of Haiti's history and culture.

The Haitian Revolution: A Story of Strength and Freedom

The people of Haiti did something that had never been done before in history they fought for their freedom and won against one of the most powerful armies in the world! Many thought it was impossible, but the Haitian people proved that with strength, courage, resilience, and faith, anything is possible.

The Haitian Revolution was the first time enslaved people stood up, defeated their masters, and created a free nation. They didn't just fight with weapons they fought with their hearts, their belief in freedom, and their unbreakable spirit. They believed that everyone deserved to be free, no matter where they came from. And even though the French army was strong, the Haitian people were stronger because they had hope, faith, and a deep connection to their ancestors.

Today, Haiti is a symbol of freedom for the world. The Haitian Revolution shows that when people unite and believe in something greater than themselves, they can overcome any challenge. The Haitian people proved that no matter how difficult things get, you can rise up, fight, and win because that's the power of belief and determination.

So, if the Haitian people could do something that had never been done before, imagine what else they can achieve! Haiti is built on strength, courage, and resilience, and that same spirit can help Haiti continue to grow into an even greater nation. Haiti has always been a symbol of freedom, and with unity and hope, it will have an even brighter future. Because when you believe in yourself, fight for what's right, and never give up, there's nothing you can't achieve. Haiti's story is proof of that!

About the Author

Born in Haiti, the author's passion for history and the story of her homeland runs deep. From an early age, her parents filled her childhood with captivating tales about Haiti's incredible past, particularly the revolutionary events that led Haiti to become the first independent Black nation in the world. Haiti's struggle for freedom and its profound impact on global history ignited a fire in the author.

After graduated from Broward College she pursued her academic journey at the Florida International University, where she earned a degree in International Relations

This degree opened her eyes to a broader view of global history, politics, and cultures, allowing her to connect the dots between Haiti's revolutionary struggle and the movements for freedom and equality around the world.

Through her work, the author has realized that many children born in the Haitian diaspora are not fully aware of the profound history that shaped their identity. Often, they know little beyond the music, food, and cultural celebrations, missing out on the deeper, transformative story of Haiti's role in world history. With this book, the author aims to change that by sharing the powerful legacy of Haiti's fight for freedom and the lasting impact it had on the world.

Her mission in writing this book is to show young readers that Haiti's story is about much more than the konpa music or delicious foods often associated with it. It is a powerful tale of resilience, bravery, and the triumph of freedom, which altered the course of humanity and continues to inspire change today.

www.ingramcontent.com/pod-product-compliance
Lightning Source LLC
Chambersburg PA
CBHW041503220426
43661CB00016B/1242